THE EDWARD DOUGLASS WHITE
LECTURES ON CITIZENSHIP

LOUISIANA STATE UNIVERSITY
1941

OTHER BOOKS BY ROBERT M. HUTCHINS

NO FRIENDLY VOICE (1936)
THE HIGHER LEARNING IN AMERICA (1936)

EDUCATION

FOR

FREEDOM

BY

ROBERT MAYNARD
HUTCHINS

LOUISIANA STATE UNIVERSITY PRESS

Baton Rouge, Louisiana

1947

To

M P M H

PREFACE

Much of the material in Chapters 2, 3, and 5 of this book was presented in the Edward Douglass White lectures at Louisiana State University in April, 1941. The authorities of the Louisiana State University Press, in addition to many other courtesies, have generously allowed me the opportunity to rewrite the lectures and have permitted me to add Chapters 1 and 4.

R. M. H.

Chicago
28 July 1942

TABLE OF CONTENTS

I

THE AUTOBIOGRAPHY OF AN UNEDUCATED MAN

I WAS born in the usual way forty-three years ago and brought up in a way that was not unusual for persons born at that time. We had morning prayers with a Bible reading every day. We went to church twice on Sunday. The result of the first is that I was amazed three weeks ago when in a class I was teaching I found a senior at the University of Chicago who had never heard of Joshua. The result of the second is that it is very hard for me to go to church now and that I find myself singing, humming, or moaning third-rate hymns like "Blest Be the Tie That Binds" while shaving, while waiting on the platform to make a speech, or in other moments of abstraction or crisis.

We had at that time many advantages that have been denied to college students in recent years, but that may be restored to their successors. We had no radios, and for all practical purposes no automobiles, no movies, and no slick-paper magazines. We had to entertain ourselves. We could not by turning a small knob or paying a small fee get somebody

I

else to do it for us. It never occurred to us that unless we could go somewhere or do something our lives were empty. We had nowhere to go, and no way to get there. Our recreations were limited to two: reading and physical exercise. The first meant reading anything you could lay your hands on. The second meant playing tennis.

You will notice that the circumstances under which I was brought up gave me some knowledge of one great book, the Bible, and the habit of reading. The habit of physical exercise I was fortunately forced to abandon at an early date. You will notice, too, that the educational system had nothing to do with any of these accomplishments or habits. I do not remember that I ever thought about being educated at all. I thought of getting through school. This, as I recall it, was a business of passing examinations and meeting requirements, all of which were meaningless to me but presumably had some meaning to those who had me in their power. I have no doubt that the Latin and Greek I studied did me good. All I can say is that I was not aware of it at the time. Nor did I have any idea of the particular kind of good it was intended to do me. Since I had got the habit of reading at home, I was perfectly willing to read anything anybody gave me. Apart from a few plays of Shakespeare nobody gave me anything good to read until I was a sophomore in college. Then I was allowed to examine the grammar and philology of the *Apology* of Socrates in a Greek course. And since I had had an unusual amount of German, I was permitted to study *Faust*.

My father once happened to remark to me that he had never liked mathematics. Since I admired my father very much, it became a point of honor with me not to like mathematics either. I finally squeezed through Solid Geometry. But when, at the age of sixteen, I entered Oberlin College, I found that the authorities felt that one hard course was all anybody ought to be asked to carry. You could take either mathematics or Greek. Of course if you took Greek you were allowed to drop Latin. I did not hesitate a moment. Languages were pie for me. It would have been unfilial to take mathematics. I took Greek, and have never seen a mathematics book since. I have been permitted to glory in the possession of an unmathematical mind.

My scientific attainments were of the same order. I had a course in physics in prep school. Every Oberlin student had to take one course in science, because every Oberlin student had to take one course in everything—in everything, that is, except Greek and mathematics. After I had blown up all the retorts in the chemistry laboratory doing the Marsh test for arsenic, the chemistry teacher was glad to give me a passing grade and let me go.

My philosophical attainments were such as may be derived from a ten weeks' course in the History of Philosophy. I do not remember anything about the course except that the book was green and that it contained pictures of Plato and Aristotle. I learned later that the pictures were wholly imaginary representations of these writers. I have some reason to believe that the contents of the books bore the same relation to their doctrines.

So I arrived at the age of eighteen and the end of my sophomore year. My formal education had given me no understanding of science, mathematics, or philosophy. It had added almost nothing to my knowledge of literature. I had some facility with languages, but today I cannot read Greek or Latin except by guesswork. What is perhaps more important, I had no idea what I was doing or why. My father was a minister and a professor. The sons of ministers and the sons of professors were supposed to go to college. College was a lot of courses. You toiled your way through those which were required and for the rest wandered around taking those that seemed most entertaining. The days of the week and the hours of the day at which courses were offered were perhaps the most important factor in determining the student's course of study.

I spent the next two years in the Army. Here I developed some knowledge of French and Italian. I learned to roll cigarettes, to blow rings, and to swear. I discovered that there was a world far from

4

Oberlin, Ohio, devoted to wine, women, and song;
but I was too well brought up even to sing.

The horrors of war are all that they are supposed
to be. They are even worse; for the worst horror
can never be written about or communicated. It is
the frightful monotony and boredom which is the lot
of the private with nothing to think about. Since my
education had given me nothing to think about, I
devoted myself, as the alternative to suicide, to the
mastery of all the arts implied in the verb "to sol-
dier." I learned to protract the performance of any
task so that I would not be asked to do another.
By the end of the war I could give the impression
that I was busy digging a ditch without putting my
pick into the ground all day. I have found this training very useful in my present capacity. But on the
whole, aside from the physiological benefits conferred upon me by a regular, outdoor life, I write
off my years in the Army as a complete blank. The
arts of soldiering, at least at the buck-private level,
are not liberal arts. The manual of arms is not a
great book.

When the war was over, I went to Yale. I thought
I would study history, because I could not study
mathematics, science, or philosophy; and history
was about all there was left. I found that the Yale
history department was on sabbatical leave. But I
found, too, that you could take your senior year in

5

the Law School with credit for the bachelor's degree. So I decided to stay two years in Yale College doing all of my last year's work in the Law School.

Yale was dissatisfied with my year of blowing up retorts in the Oberlin chemistry laboratory. Yale said I had to take another science; any science would do. Discussion with my friends revealed the fact that the elementary course in biology was not considered difficult even for people like me. I took that and spent a good deal of time in the laboratory cutting up frogs. I don't know why. I can tell you nothing now about the inside of a frog. In addition to the laboratory we had lectures. All I remember about them is that the lecturer lectured with his eyes closed. He was the leading expert in the country on the paramecium. We all believed that he lectured with his eyes closed because he had to stay up all night watching the paramecia reproduce. Beyond this experience Yale imposed no requirements on me, and I wandered aimlessly round until senior year.

In that year I did all my work in the Law School, except that I had to obey a regulation of obscure origin and purpose which compelled every Yale College student working in the Law School to take one two-hour course in the College. I took a two-hour course in American Literature because it was the only two-hour course in the College which came at twelve o'clock. A special advantage of this course was that the instructor, who was much in demand as a lecturer to popular audiences, often had to leave at 12:20 to make the 12:29 for New York.

I see now that my formal education began in the Law School. My formal education began, that is, at the age of twenty-one. I do not mean to say that I knew then that I was getting an education. I am sure the professors did not know they were giving me one. They would have been shocked at such an insinuation. They thought they were teaching me law. They did not teach me any law. But they did something far more important: they introduced me to the liberal arts.

It is sad but true that the only place in an American university where the student is taught to read, write, and speak is the law school. The principal, if not the sole, merit of the case method of instruction is that the student is compelled to read accurately and carefully, to state accurately and carefully the meaning of what he has read, to criticize the reasoning of opposing cases, and to write very extended examinations in which the same standards of accuracy, care, and criticism are imposed. It is too bad that this experience is limited to very few students and that those few arrive at the stage where they may avail themselves of it only at about age twenty-two. It is unfortunate that the teachers have no training in the liberal arts as such. The whole thing is on a rough-and-ready basis, but it is grammar, rhetoric, and logic just the same, and a good deal better than none at all.

One may regret, too, that the materials upon which these disciplines are employed are no more significant than they are. No case book is a great book. Not more than two or three judges in the history of Anglo-American law have been great writers. One who is immersed long enough in the turgidities of some of the masters of the split infinitive who have graced the American bench may eventually come to write like them.

One may regret as well that no serious attempt is made in the law schools to have the student learn anything about the intellectual history of the intellectual content of the law. At only one law school that I know of is it thought important to connect the law with ethics and politics. In most law schools there is a course in Jurisprudence. At Yale in my day it was an elective one-semester course in the last year, and was ordinarily taken by about ten students. Still, the Yale Law School did begin my formal education. Though it was too little and too late, it was something, and I shall always be grateful for it.

After I graduated from college and ended my first year of law I took a year and a half off and taught English and History in a preparatory school. This continued my education in the liberal arts. I did not learn any history, because the school was solely interested in getting boys through the College Board Examinations. We taught from textbooks, usually the most compact we could find, for we were reasonably sure that if the boys had memorized what was in the textbook they could pass the examinations. We did not allow them to read anything except the textbook for fear of confusing their minds.

But in teaching, and especially in teaching English Composition, I discovered that there were rules of reading, writing, and speaking, and that it was worth while to learn them, and even to try to teach them. I came to suspect, for the first time, that my teachers in school had had something in mind. I began to fall into a dangerous heresy, the heresy that since the best way to learn something is to teach it, the only way to learn anything is to teach it. I am sure that in what is called "the curriculum" of the conventional school, college, or university the only people who are getting an education are the teachers. They work in more or less coherent, if somewhat narrow, fields, and they work in more or less intelligible ways. The student, on the other hand, works through a multifarious collection of disconnected courses in such a way that the realms of knowledge are likely to become less and less intelligible as he proceeds. In such an institution the only way to learn anything is to teach it. The difficulty with this procedure is that in the teacher's early years, at least, it is likely to make the education of his students even worse than it would otherwise have been.

After continuing my education in the liberal arts in this rather unpleasant and inefficient way, I returned to Yale at the age of twenty-three, became an officer of the University, and finished my law work out of hours. Just before I was about to graduate from the Law School at the age of twenty-six, a man who was scheduled to teach in the School that summer got appendicitis, and a substitute had to be found. Since I was already on the pay roll and everybody else was out of town, I became a member of the faculty of the Law School.

Here I continued my education in the liberal arts, this time unconsciously, for I was no more aware than the rest of the faculty that the liberal arts were what we were teaching. At the end of my first year of this the man who was teaching the law of Evidence resigned, and, because of my unusual qualifications, I was put in his place. My qualifications were that I had never studied the subject, in or out of law school, and that I knew nothing of the disciplines on which the law of Evidence is founded, namely psychology and logic.

The law of Evidence bothered me. I couldn't understand what made it go. There is a rule, for example, that evidence of flight from the scene of a crime is admissible as tending to show guilt. After painful research the only foundation I could find for this was the statement, emanating, I grant, from the very highest source, that the wicked flee when no man pursueth, but the righteous are as bold as a lion.

There is a rule which admits, as worthy the attention of the jury, utterances made immediately after a blow on the head, or after any sudden shock, such as having somebody say "boo" to you. As far as I could discover, this doctrine rested on the psychological principle, long held incontrovertible, that a blow on the head or having somebody say "boo" to him prevents even the habitual liar, momentarily but effectually, from indulging in the practice of his art. Since I was supposed to lead my students to the knowledge of what the rules ought to be, and not merely of what they were, I wanted to find out whether the wicked really do flee when no man pursueth, whether the righteous really are as bold as a lion, and whether you really can startle a liar out of his disregard for the truth.

It was obviously impossible to conduct controlled experiments on these interesting questions. I could not think about them, because I had had no education. The psychologists and logicians I met could not think about them, because they had had no education either. I could think about legal problems as legal. They could think about psychological problems as psychological. I didn't know how to think about legal problems as psychological; they didn't know how to think about psychological problems as legal. Finally I heard that there was a young psychologist, logician, and philosopher at Columbia by the name of Adler who was actually examining the bible of all Evidence teachers, the seven volumes of *Wigmore on Evidence*. A man who was willing to make such sacrifices deserved investigation, and I got in touch with Mr. Adler right away.

I found that Mr. Adler was just as uneducated as I was, but that he had begun to get over it, and to do so in a way that struck me as very odd. He had been teaching for several years in John Erskine's Honors Course in the Great Books at Columbia. I paid no attention and went on trying to find out how I could put a stopwatch on the return of power to lie after a blow on the head.

I now transport you forward four years, from 1925—to 1929. I am President of the University of Chicago. Mr. Adler is a member of the faculty of the University of Chicago. We had fled from New Haven and New York, and we must have been guilty, for we had fled when I assure you no man had any idea of pursuing us. By this time Mr. Adler had had four more years with the Great Books at Columbia. He looked on me, my work, my education, and my prospects and found us not good. He had discovered that merely reading was not enough. He had found out that the usefulness of reading was some way related to the excellence of what was read and the plan for reading it. I knew that reading was a good thing, but had hitherto been under the impression that it didn't make any difference what you read or how it was related to anything else you read. I had arrived at the age of thirty, you will remember, with some knowledge of the Bible, of Shakespeare, of *Faust,* of one dialogue of Plato, and of the opinions of many semiliterate and a few literate judges, and that was about all. Mr. Adler further represented to me that the sole reading matter of university presidents was the telephone book. He intimated that unless I did something drastic I would close my educational career a wholly uneducated man. He broadly hinted that the president of an educational institution ought to have some education. For two years we discussed these matters, and then, at the age of thirty-two, my education began in earnest.

For eleven years we have taught the Great Books in various parts of the University: in University High School, in the College, in the Humanities Division, in the Law School, in the Department of Education, in University College, the extension division, four hours a week three quarters of the year. All this and the preparation for it has had to be carried on between board meetings, faculty meetings, committee meetings, conferences, trips, speeches, money-raising efforts, and attempts to abolish football, to award the B.A. at the end of the sophomore year, and otherwise to wreck the educational system. Thanks to the kind co-operation of the students, I have made some progress with my education. In my more optimistic moments I flatter myself that I have arrived at about the stage which I think the American sophomore should have reached. But this is an exaggeration. The American sophomore, to qualify for the bachelor's degree, should not be ignorant of mathematics and science.

Now what I want to know is why I should have had to wait until age forty-three to get an education somewhat worse than that which any sophomore ought to have. The liberal arts are the arts of freedom. To be free a man must understand the tradition in which he lives. A great book is one which yields up through the liberal arts a clear and important understanding of our tradition. An education which consisted of the liberal arts as understood through great books and of great books understood through the liberal arts would be one and the only one which would enable us to comprehend the tradition in which we live. It must follow that if we want to educate our students for freedom, we must educate them in the liberal arts and in the great books. And this education we must give them, not by the age of forty-three, but by the time they are eighteen, or at the latest twenty.

We have been so preoccupied with trying to find

out how to teach everybody to read anything that we have forgotten the importance of what is read. Yet it is obvious that if we succeeded in teaching everybody to read, and everybody read nothing but pulp magazines, obscene literature, and *Mein Kampf,* the last state of the nation would be worse than the first. Literacy is not enough.

The common answer is that the great books are too difficult for the modern pupil. All I can say is that it is amazing how the number of too difficult books has increased in recent years. The books that are now too difficult for candidates for the doctorate were the regular fare of grammar-school boys in the Middle Ages and the Renaissance. Most of the great books of the world were written for ordinary people, not for professors alone. Mr. Adler and I have found that the books are more rather than less effective the younger the students are. Students in University High School have never heard that these books are too hard for them and that they shouldn't read them. They have not had time to get as miseducated as their elders. They read the books and like them because they think they are good books about important matters. The experience at St. John's College, in the Humanities General Course at Columbia, in the General Courses of the College of the University of Chicago, and the University of Chicago College course known as Reading, Writing, and Criticism is the same.

Ask any foreign scholar you meet what he thinks about American students. He will tell you that they are eager and able to learn, that they will respond to the best that is offered them, but that they are miserably trained and dreadfully unenlightened. If you put these two statements together you can come to only one conclusion, and that is that it is not the inadequacy of the students but the inadequacy of the environment and the irresolution of teachers that is responsible for the shortcomings of American education.

So Quintilian said: "For there is absolutely no foundation for the complaint that but few men have the power to take in the knowledge that is imparted to them, and that the majority are so slow of understanding that education is a waste of time and labor. On the contrary you will find that most are quick to reason and ready to learn. Reasoning comes as naturally to man as flying to birds, speed to horses and ferocity to beasts of prey: our minds are endowed by nature with such activity and sagacity that the soul is believed to proceed from heaven. Those who are dull and unteachable are as abnormal as prodigious births and monstrosities, and are but few in number. A proof of what I say is to be found in the fact that boys commonly show promise of many accomplishments, and when such promise dies away as they grow up, this is plainly due not to the failure of natural gifts, but to lack of the requisite

16

care. But, it will be urged, there are degrees of talent. Undoubtedly, I reply, and there will be a corresponding variation in actual accomplishment: but that there are any who gain nothing from education, I absolutely deny."

When we remember that only a little more than 1500 years ago the ancestors of most of us, many of them painted blue, were roaming the trackless forests of Caledonia, Britain, Germany, and transalpine Gaul, despised by the civilized citizens of Rome and Antioch, interested, in the intervals of rapine, only in deep drinking and high gaming; savage, barbarous, cruel, and illiterate, we may reflect with awe and expectation on the potentialities of our race. When we remember, too, that it is only a little more than fifty years ago that the "average man" began to have the chance to get an education, we must recognize that it is too early to despair of him.

The President of Dalhousie has correctly said, "Over most of Europe the books and monuments have been destroyed and bombed. To destroy European civilization in America you do not need to burn its records in a single fire. Leave those records unread for a few generations and the effect will be the same."

The alternatives before us are clear. Either we must abandon the ideal of freedom or we must educate our people for freedom. If an education in the liberal arts and in the great books is the education for freedom, then we must make the attempt to give this education to all our citizens. And since it is a long job, and one upon which the fate of our country in war and peace may depend, we shall have to start now.

II

THE AIMS OF EDUCATION

SIX years ago I had the honor of addressing my fellow Yale men on the Higher Learning in America. I was surprised to find that these lectures did not have the effect they were intended to produce. Instead, all the movements they were designed to arrest, all the attitudes they were calculated to change, went rushing onward, in the case of the movements, or became more firmly entrenched, in the case of the attitudes.

I attacked triviality, and forty-two students enrolled in the Oklahoma University short course for drum majors.

I attacked vocationalism, and the University of California announced a course in cosmetology, saying, "The profession of beautician is the fastest growing in this state."

I deplored a curriculum of obsolescent information, and one of America's most distinguished sociologists announced that our information was increasing so rapidly that in order to get time to pour it all into our students we should have to prolong adolescence at least until age forty-five.

I asserted that higher education was primarily

intellectual, and the President of the New York State College for Teachers said, "Education is not even primarily intellectual, certainly not chiefly intellectual. It is the process by which the emotions are socialized."

I lamented the confusion that besets American education, and the President of a highly confused and very large college announced that chaos was a good thing. Though I should prefer chaos to an order imposed by force, I had never supposed that chaos was an ideal toward which all right-thinking men should strive. Chaos had always seemed to me something you tried to get out of. I had always thought that what we wanted, both in politics and education, was a rational order, rationally arrived at.

One professor accidentally agreed with me. He made the following outrageous remarks in a book of his own: "There will always remain," he said, "certain permanent values which education must cultivate, such as intellectual honesty, love of truth, ability to think clearly, moral qualities." The fact that he was from Teachers College, Columbia, and could be assumed to be only teasing, did not save him. He was sharply rebuked by a professor from Ohio State University who said that here he must "part company with the author of this indisputably significant volume, for the suspicion grows that the author is still something of an absolutist." The author actually wanted education to cultivate intellectual honesty, the love of truth, the ability to think clearly, and moral qualities.

Now I will not deny that one or two people did pay some attention to my book. They had to. And they got it free in the course of their trade as book reviewers. One of these, who in his spare time is a professor at Yale, summed up the whole thing by saying that the trouble with me was my intense moral idealism. Such a quality would naturally distort anybody's view of education. A university president guilty of moral idealism? What is the world coming to? By some process of association of ideas I am reminded of the remarks of one of our alumni who in a recent discussion at the University of Chicago said that everything I had said about football was logical, perfectly logical, very logical indeed. "But," he said, "if the University abolishes football, my son, now fifteen years old, will not want to go there." In other words, "logical" is a term of reproach, and the University of Chicago should be illogical because one of its alumni has an illogical child. I have even heard the word "educational" in the same slurring connotation, as when a Princeton graduate wrote to Woodrow Wilson saying, "I will have nothing more to do with Princeton. You are turning my dear old college into an educational institution." A university president who is suspected of an interest in morals, in intellect, or even in education deserves the severest condemnation from those who have the true interests of our country at heart.

But all these things are as nothing compared with the menace of metaphysics. I had mildly suggested that metaphysics might unify the modern university. I knew it was a long word, but I thought my audience of learned reviewers would know what it meant. I was somewhat surprised to find that to them metaphysics was a series of balloons, floating far above the surface of the earth, which could be pulled down by vicious or weak-minded people when they wanted to win an argument. The explosion of one of these balloons or the release of the gases it contained might silence, but never convince, a wise man. The wise man would go away muttering, "Words, words, words," or "Antiscientific," "Reactionary," or even "Fascist." Knowing that there is nothing true unless experimental science makes it so, the wise man knows that metaphysics is simply a technical name for superstition.

Now I might as well make a clean breast of it all. I am interested in education, in morals, in intellect, and in metaphysics. I even go so far as to hold that there is a necessary relation among all these things. I am willing to assert that without one we cannot have the others and that without the others we cannot have the one with which I am primarily concerned, namely education.

I insist, moreover, that everything that is happening in the world today confirms the immediate and pressing necessity of pulling ourselves together and getting ourselves straight on these matters. The world is probably closer to disintegration now than at any time since the fall of the Roman Empire. If there are any forces of clarification and unification left, however slight and ineffectual they may appear, they had better be mobilized instantly, or all that we have known as Western Civilization may vanish.

Even assuming that normal conditions will soon be restored, we must grant that our country has long been afflicted with problems which, though apparently insoluble, must be solved if this nation is to be preserved or to be worth preserving. These problems are not material problems. We may have faith that the vast resources of our land and the technological genius of our people will produce a supply of material goods adequate for the maintenance of that interesting fiction, the American Standard of Living. No, our problems are moral, intellectual, and spiritual. The paradox of starvation in the midst of plenty illustrates the nature of our difficulties. This paradox will not be resolved by technical skill or scientific data. It will be resolved, if it is resolved at all, by wisdom and goodness.

Now wisdom and goodness are the aim of higher education. How can it be otherwise? Wisdom and goodness are the end of human life. If you dispute this, you are at once entering upon a metaphysical controversy; for you are disputing about the nature of being and the nature of man. This is as it should be. How can we consider man's destiny unless we ask what he is? How can we talk about preparing men for life unless we ask what the end of life may be? At the base of education, as at the base of every human activity, lies metaphysics.

So it is with science. As Dr. H. S. Burr of the Yale Medical School has put it: "One of the primitive assumptions of science is that we live in a universe of order; order determined by, and controlled through, the operation of fundamental principles capable of elucidation and reasonably exact definition. This assumption states that there is a metaphysics, a body of universal laws which can be grasped by the human intellect and utilized effectively in the solution of human problems."

So it is with ethics and politics. We want to lead the good life. We want the good state as a means to that life. Once more, to find the good life and the good state, we must inquire into the nature of man and the ends of life. The minute we do that we are metaphysicians in spite of ourselves. Moreover, if ethics is the science of human freedom, we must know at the beginning whether and in what sense man is free. Here we are metaphysicians once again. And the soundness of our moral conclusions depends on whether we are good metaphysicians or bad ones. So the more preposterous positions of Mill's *Essay on Liberty* originate in his mistaken or inadequate analysis of the doctrine of free will; and Aristotle's defense of natural slavery results from his failure to remember that according to Aristotelian metaphysics there can be no such thing as a natural slave.

So it is with education. Here the great criminal was Mr. Eliot, who as President of Harvard applied his genius, skill, and longevity to the task of robbing American youth of their cultural heritage. Since he held that there were no such things as good or bad subjects of study, his laudable effort to open the curriculum to good ones naturally led him to open it to bad ones and finally to destroy it altogether. Today, though it is possible to get an education in an American university, a man would have to be so bright and know so much to get it that he wouldn't really need it. Our institutions give full support to the proposition of Gibbon that "instruction is seldom of much efficacy except in those happy dispositions in which it is almost superfluous." Today the young American comprehends only by accident the intellectual tradition of which he is a part and in which he must live: for its scattered and disjointed fragments are strewn from one end of the campus to the other. Our university graduates have far more information and far less understanding than in the colonial period. And our universities present themselves to our people in this crisis either as rather ineffectual trade schools or as places where nice boys and girls have a nice time under the supervision of nice men and women in a nice environment.

The crucial error is that of holding that nothing is any more important than anything else, that there can be no order of goods and no order in the intellectual realm. There is nothing central and nothing peripheral, nothing primary and nothing secondary, nothing basic and nothing superficial. The course of study goes to pieces because there is nothing to hold it together. Triviality, mediocrity, and vocationalism take it over because we have no standard by which to judge them. We have little to offer as a substitute for a sound curriculum except talk of personality, "character," and great teachers, the slogans of educational futilitarianism.

We see, then, that metaphysics plays a double part in higher education. By way of their metaphysics educators determine what education they shall offer. By way of metaphysics their students must lay the foundations of their moral, intellectual, and spiritual life. By way of metaphysics I arrive at the conclusion that the aim of education is wisdom and goodness and that studies which do not bring us closer to this goal have no place in a university. If you have a different opinion, you must show that you have a better metaphysics. By way of metaphysics, students, on their part, may recover a rational view of the universe and of their role in it. If you deny this proposition you take the responsibility of asserting that a rational view of the universe and one's role in it is no better than an irrational one or none at all.

Let us, in the light of these principles, look at the relation of education to the improvement of society. We all want to improve society, and we want college graduates because of their education to want to improve society and to know how to do it. Differences appear when we come to the method by which these educational objects may be attained. Since the issue before us is education, I shall not attempt to deal with the problem of how a university may through its scientific investigations best prevent or cure soil erosion, juvenile delinquency, or war. I shall discuss only the method by which an institution may develop in its students a social consciousness and a social conscience.

At first glance it would seem that we should all agree that in order to talk about society or its improvement we should have to inquire into the nature of society, into the common and abiding characteristics of society, and of those unusual animals who compose it, namely men. We should want to consider the history of societies, their rise, development, and decay. We should wish to examine their object, the various ways of achieving it, and the degree to which each succeeded or failed. In order

27

to talk about success or failure we should have to have some notions about what a good society was. Without such notions we could not appraise the societies that came under our eye or the one in which we lived. We should need to have some conception of a good society in order to decide what improvement was; for we all know that we have welcomed many measures as beneficent which when adopted have seemed to leave us in as unsatisfactory condition as we were in before. In short, if we approached the great task of improving society without prejudice, we should think at once of trying to understand the nature, the purpose, and the history of the institutions which man has created. The quest for social improvement is a perpetual quest. Ever since societies existed men have been trying to make them better. The ideas and the experience of mankind should, one would think, be placed in the hands of the rising generation as it goes forward on the perpetual quest.

This would mean that if we wanted a student to have a sense of social responsibility and the desire to live up to his obligations we should have to give him, to achieve this aim, whatever we gave him for other purposes—an education in history and philosophy, together with the disciplines needed to understand those fields. For the purpose of making him an improver of society we should hope to make him, in a modest way, master of the political wisdom of the race. Without some inkling of it he could not understand a social problem. He could not criticize a social institution. He would be without the weapons needed to attack or to defend one. He could not tell a good one from a bad one. He could not think intelligently about one.

It is hardly necessary for me to add that nobody can think about a practical problem like the problem of improving society unless he knows the facts. He cannot comment usefully on the situation in Germany unless he knows what the situation is. Neither can he do so unless he has some standard of criticism and of action. This standard cannot, of course, be a mathematical formula or some miraculous automatic intellectual gadget which when applied to the facts will immediately and infallibly produce the right answer. The practical world is a world of contingent singular things and not a mathematical system. No one has emphasized this point more forcefully than Aristotle. But this did not restrain him from attempting in the *Ethics* and *Politics* to work out the general principles of the good life and the good state, or from trying to show the utility of such principles in his society and, as I think, in any other.

If, then, we are to have standards of social criticism and social action, and if they are to be anything but emotional standards, they must result from philosophical and historical study and from the habit of straight thinking therein. It would be a wonderful

29

Disguised Marxism
or an attempt
to enter an
economic
criticism in a
time soon to
be "red scared".

thing if we were all so conditioned that our reflexes worked unanimously in the right direction when confronted by political and economic injustice, if we could be trained in infancy to recognize and fight it. But even if we could arrive at adolescence in this happy state I am afraid that our excellent habits might fall away under pressure. Something is needed to preserve them, and this is understanding. This is another way of saying that the intellect commands the will. Our parents should make every effort in our childhood to moderate our passions and to habituate us to justice and prudence. But the role of higher education in this connection must be to supply the firm and enduring groundwork to sustain these habits when the tumult of adult life beats upon them.

It seems obvious to me, therefore, that the kind of education I have been urging is the kind that helps to develop a social consciousness and a social conscience. Why isn't it obvious to everybody else? The first reason, I think, is the popularity of the cult of skepticism. I have been saying that I want to give the student knowledge about society. But we have got ourselves into such a state of mind that if anybody outside of natural science says he knows anything, he is a dogmatist and an authoritarian. Anybody who says, "I don't know because nobody can"; or, "Everything is a matter of opinion"; or, "I will take no position because I am tolerant and openminded" is a liberal, progressive, democratic fellow to whom the fate of the world may safely be entrusted.

I regret that I am forced to remind you that the two most eminent skeptics of modern times were among its most stalwart reactionaries. Hume was a Tory of the deepest dye, and Montaigne was, too. This was a perfectly natural consequence of their philosophical position. Montaigne held, in effect, that "there was nothing more dangerous than to touch a political order once it had been established. For who knows whether the next will be better? The world is living by custom and tradition; we should not disturb it on the strength of private opinions which express little more than our own moods and humors, or, at the utmost the local prejudices of our own country." The decision to which the skepticism of Hume and Montaigne led them was the decision to let the world alone. There is another decision to which they could have come and at which others of their faith have actually arrived. If we can know nothing about society, if we can have only opinion about it, and if one man's opinion is as good as another's, then we may decide to get what we irrationally want by the use of irrational means, namely force. The appeal to reason is vain in a skeptical world. That appeal can only be successful if those appealed to have some rational views of the society of which they are a part.

A second reason why some people doubt the social

utility of the education I favor is that they belong
to the cult of immediacy, or of what may be called
presentism. In this view the way to comprehend the
world is to grapple with the reality you find about
you. You tour the stockyards and the steel plants
and understand the industrial system. There is no
past. Any reference to antiquity or the Middle Ages
shows that you are not interested in social progress.
Philosophy is merely a function of its time and place.
We live in a different time and usually a different
place. Hence philosophers who lived yesterday have
nothing to say to us today.

But we cannot understand the environment by
looking at it. It presents itself to us as a mass of
incomprehensible items. Simply collecting these
items does not enlighten us. It may lead only to that
worship of information which, according to John
Dewey, still curses the social studies, and understanding escapes us still. We attack old problems
not knowing they are old and make the same mistakes because we do not know they were made. So
Stuart Chase and Thurman Arnold some years ago
renewed the mediaeval controversy between the
nominalists and the realists without showing that
they realized that the subject had ever been discussed before or that they had the knowledge or
training to conduct the discussion to any intelligible
end.

The method of disposing of philosophy by placing

it in a certain time and then saying that time is gone has been adequately dealt with by a contemporary historian. He says, "It ascribes the birth of Aristotelianism to the fact that Aristotle was a Greek and a pagan, living in a society based on slavery, four centuries before Christ; it also explains the revival of Aristotelianism in the thirteenth century by the fact that St. Thomas Aquinas was an Italian, a Christian, and even a monk, living in a feudal society, whose political and economic structure was widely different from that of the fourth-century Greece; and it accounts equally well for the Aristotelianism of J. Maritain, who is French, a layman, and living in the 'bourgeois' society of a nineteenth-century republic. Conversely, since they were living in the same times and the same places, just as Aristotle should have held the same philosophy as Plato, so Abelard and St. Bernard, St. Bonaventure and St. Thomas Aquinas, Descartes and Gassendi, all these men, who flatly contradicted one another, should have said more or less the same things."

You will see at once that skepticism and presentism are related to a third ism that distorts our view of the method of education for social improvement. This is the cult of scientism, a cult to which, curiously enough, very few natural scientists belong. It is a cult composed of those who misconceive the nature or the role of science. They say that science is modern; science is tentative; science is progressive.

33

Everything which is not science is antiquated, or at best irrelevant. A writer in so respectable and learned a publication as the *International Journal of Ethics* has called upon us to follow science in our quest for the good life, and the fact that he is a philosopher suggests that the cult of scientism has found members in the most unlikely places. For it must be clear that though we can and should use science to achieve social improvement, we cannot follow it to this destination. The reason is that science does not tell us where to go. Men may employ it for good or evil purposes; but it is the men that have the purposes, and they do not learn them from their scientific studies.

Scientism is a disservice to science. The rise of science is the most important fact of modern life. No student should be permitted to complete his education without understanding it. Universities should and must support and encourage scientific research. From a scientific education we may expect an understanding of science. From scientific investigation we may expect scientific knowledge. We are confusing the issue and demanding what we have no right to ask if we seek to learn from science the goals of human life and of organized society.

Finally, we have the cult of anti-intellectualism, which has some oddly assorted members. They range from Hitler, who thinks with his red corpuscles, through the members of the three other cults, to men of good will, who, since they are men of good will, are at the opposite pole to Hitler, but can give no rational justification for being there. They hold that philosophy of the heart which Auguste Comte first celebrated. Comte belonged to the cult of scientism. Therefore he could know nothing but what science told him. But he wanted social improvement. Hence he tried to make a philosophy and finally a religion out of science, and succeeded only in producing something which was no one of the three and which was, in fact, little more than sentimentalism.

Sentimentalism is an irrational desire to be helpful to one's fellow men. It sometimes appears as an ingratiating and even a redeeming quality in those who cannot or will not think. But the sentimentalist is really a dangerous character. He distrusts the intellect, because it might show him he is wrong. He believes in the primacy of the will, and this is what makes him dangerous. You don't know what you ought to want; you don't know why you want what you want. But you do know that you want it. This easily develops into the notion that since you want it, you ought to have it. You are a man of good will, and your opponents by definition are not. Since you ought to have what you want, you should get it if you have the power; and here the journey from the man of good will to Hitler is complete.

This is indeed the position in which the members of all four cults—skepticism, presentism, scientism,

35

and anti-intellectualism—find themselves on questions of social improvement. Since they cannot know, they must feel. We can only hope that they will feel good. But we cannot be very hopeful. Where does the good will come from? Long ago the campaign before the Austrian plebiscite gave us the news for the first time that Hitler was guided by a special revelation. Most other men of good will do not claim such intimate contact with the Deity. But they are uniformly mysterious about the source of their inspiration. If it is not knowledge, and hence in this case philosophy, it must be habit—habit of the most irrational kind. A university can have nothing to do with irrational habits, except to try to moderate the bad ones and support the good ones. But if by hypothesis we cannot do this by rational means, we are forced to the conclusion that a university must be a large nursery school tenderly preserving good habits from shock, in the hope that if they can be nursed long enough they will last through life, though without any rational foundation. In this view the boarding school in the country would be the only proper training ground for American youth, and the University of Chicago could take no part in social improvement. In fact, it would be a subversive institution.

It hardly helps us here to say, as many anti-intellectuals do, that education must educate "the whole man." Of all the meaningless phrases in educational discussion this is the prize. Does it mean that education must do the whole job of translating the whole infant into a whole adult? Must it do what the church, the family, the state, the Y.M.C.A., and the Boy Scouts allege they are trying to do? If so, what is the place of these important or interesting organizations, and what becomes of that intellectual training which educational institutions might be able to give if they could get around to it? Are we compelled to assume that our students can learn nothing from life or that they have led no life before coming to us and lead none after they come? Moreover, what we are seeking is a guide to the emphasis that higher education must receive. Talk of the whole man seems to imply that there should be no emphasis at all. All "parts" of the man are of equal importance: his dress, his food, his health, his family, his business. Is education to emphasize them all? That would be like saying, if we were going to study the war, that in studying it we should emphasize the war. A flat equality among subjects, interests, and powers will hardly lead to the satisfactory development of any. Is it too much to say that if we can teach our students to lead the life of reason we shall do all that can be expected of us and do at the same time the best thing that can be done for the whole man? The task of education is to make rational animals more perfectly rational.

We see, then, that the quest for social improvement is a perpetual one. Men have always wanted not a different society, but a better one. What a better society is and how to get it has been one of the persistent problems of philosophy and one of the fundamental issues in the tradition of the Western World. Only those who recognize the important place that philosophy and the wisdom of the race must hold in education for citizenship can hope to educate men and women who can contribute to the improvement of society and who will want to do so. The cults of skepticism, presentism, scientism, and anti-intellectualism will lead us to despair, not merely of education, but also of society.

III

MATERIALISM AND ITS
CONSEQUENCES

WE see the world in which we shall have to live going to pieces before our eyes. Europe as we have known it seems fated to disappear. The repercussions of the war upon our political and economic life are bound to be severe and may drastically alter the political and economic structure in which we have been brought up. We are under a duty to inquire into the first causes of the catastrophe, into the methods of averting its most serious consequences, and into the foundations of the new order which the survivors should seek to lay.

It will not be enough to examine these questions in terms of the relocation of boundaries and the redistribution of power. We cannot be content with a rearrangement of things in the material order. At the root of the present troubles of the world we must find a pervasive materialism, a devastating desire for material goods, which sweeps everything before it, up to, and perhaps over, the verge of the abyss. Since the desire for material goods is unlimited, it cannot possibly be satisfied. Everybody cannot pos-

39

sibly have everything he wants. Some nations must be denied some things they want and must inevitably try to wrest them from other nations. As long as this spirit prevails, rearrangements of things in the material order must be temporary. They will last only so long as it takes the defeated nations to recuperate and enter upon a new trial of strength.

We know now that mechanical and technical progress is not identical with civilization. We must conclude, in fact, that our faith that technology will take the place of justice has been naïve. Technology supplies the goods we want, for material goods are indubitably goods. Technology can give us bigger, brighter, faster, and cheaper automobiles. It cannot tell us who ought to have them, or how many, or where they should go. The notion that a just and equitable distribution of goods will be achieved by the advance of technology or that by its aid we shall put material goods in their proper relation to all others is reduced to absurdity by the coincidence of the zenith of technology and the nadir of moral and political life.

The doctrine by which we have lived is that material goods are an end in themselves. Hence all activity is judged by the profits it brings. The principle is that of the largest returns at the lowest costs. The criterion is purely economic. All extraeconomic or noneconomic standards, since they impede the struggle toward the goal, must be obliterated. Thus slavery was justified because it lowered costs, and attacked because it was unfair competition. The exploitation of women and children was defended because it paid. The family could not be allowed to block the path of "progress." The state is valuable if it helps to maximize profits, but is apparently to have little part in economic life beyond this and beyond fulfilling functions which are too big or too unprofitable for private enterprise. Even patriotism and the love of country fall before the onslaught, as in the case of the international money-maker in Ancient Greece who, when asked what country he belonged to, replied, "I am one of the rich."

This is the process of economic rationalization, the process of looking at everything in economic terms and testing everything by economic criteria. Even the institution of property, often mistaken for the sign of a materialistic civilization, may disappear before the advance of economic rationalization. As an Italian economist has pointed out, the most technically perfect economic realization of materialism "is the Soviet system, in which all private and public efforts have only one end: the economic rationalization of the whole of life, to the point of abolishing private property and the family, and of attempting the destruction of all religious ideals that might threaten such materialistic rationalization." Communism does not reject the mechanization of life; it completes it. It does not deny that economic activity is the principal basis of civilization; it asserts that it is the sole basis. It does not oppose huge concentrations of economic power; on the contrary, in order to facilitate and control the work of concentration, it accumulates all capital and concentrates all economic life in the hands of the state. Russian communism is simply the logical prolongation of capitalistic materialism.

Materialism has captured our culture. It has captured the state. It has captured education; for no one will deny that the test of education is whether the graduates succeed in life, and even those who argue for intellectual development as the aim of education are constrained to add that the man with a developed intellect will make more money than the man with an undeveloped one.

The educational creed offered by S. R. Livingstone, Director of Personnel of the Thompson Products Company, commands the general agreement he claims for it. He says, "I think most of us will agree generally with this broad statement—that the purpose of education is primarily and basically to equip young people with knowledge and skill by means of which they can most effectively contribute to the production of food, clothing, shelter, and the luxuries which go to make up our standard of living. While knowledge of such fields as the arts, languages, philosophy, history, and others is of importance to society, still I believe these fields are secondary, at least at this time, to the production of the material necessities and luxuries, as society is now demonstrating that it cannot be happy without an abundance of the material things."

As materialism has taken over education, so it has taken over morals. It has retained the names of the Christian virtues and changed their meaning to suit its purposes. Mr. Kimpton, the jeweler in the town where I was brought up, had a sign in his window saying, "Honesty is the best policy, because it pays." Courage is the nerve it takes to run business risks. Temperance means saving your money and staying in good working condition. Prudence is just another name for shrewdness. These translations suggest that moral criteria have departed, to have their places taken by economic criteria.

Yet, now that the triumph of materialism is complete, now that we are all agreed that religion is good for the people, and relief is needed to keep them quiet, and education to teach them to consume and produce, and the family to attach them to their work, and the state to act as the guarantor of an independent, autonomous economic machine—the world this spirit has made is collapsing about us, and this spirit offers us nothing but gold, with which we cannot buy salvation.

It would be laughable to try to build a new order with the old ideals. As Maritain has put it, if we *Maritain* would change the face of the earth, we must first change our own hearts. We are concerned, not with a rearrangement of material things, but with a moral and spiritual reformation. This reformation must be intellectual, too; for it requires the substitution of rational views of man, the state, and the order of goods for irrational or subrational ones. Without pretending to any special revelation, let us see whether we can make some tentative and hesitant approaches to the lines which a moral, intellectual, and spiritual revolution might follow.

Man is a moral, rational, and spiritual being. He needs material goods; unless he has them he cannot survive. But he does not need them without limit. Preoccupation with material goods will hinder and not assist his progress toward his real goal, which is the fullest development of his specific powers. Nature will not forgive those who fail to fulfill the law of their being. The law of human beings is wisdom and goodness, not unlimited acquisition. The economic rationalization of life proceeds in the face of the basic law of human nature. That law would suggest to us the idea of sufficiency rather than the idea of unbounded possessions.

The economic rationalization of life, moreover, proceeds in the face of the basic law of human society. Men are banded together in society for mutual aid toward the objectives of their personal lives, which are, as we have seen, the development of their highest powers. As John Stuart Mill said, "The

44

most important point of excellence which any form of government can possess is to promote the virtue and the intelligence of the people." The state is not an end in itself, but a means to the virtue and intelligence, that is the happiness, of the citizens. It is held together by justice, through which it cares for the common good. The common good, in fact, is little but justice most broadly conceived: peace, order, and an equitable distribution of economic goods. Since the state is charged with responsibility for the common good, and since the production and distribution of material goods are one aspect of the common good, the economic order must be subordinate to the political order.

The economic rationalization of life makes the political order subordinate to the economic order or confuses the two. We can see this in any campaign, when each candidate tells the citizens of the financial rewards they will reap by voting for him. We are accustomed to saying in the same breath that the government must let economic activity alone and that it must see to it that the particular economic activity in which we are engaged prospers. So we look upon our neighbor either as a customer or a competitor or an instrument of production. The eminent dignity of human beings forbids us, even if the two great commandments did not, to look upon our neighbor in any of these ways, and particularly to regard him as a means of enriching ourselves.

In this setting we may understand the institution of property. Since man is an artist, an animal that makes things, the individual man is entitled to a sense of participation in the ownership of the instruments of production and in the goods produced. But since the earth was given to man and not to individual men, since man is a social and political animal with social responsibilities, one who acquires property beyond the needs of himself and his family must dedicate it to social purposes. This is the rule of reason, which is nothing but the idea of sufficiency. It is the opposite of the idea of unlimited gain. A violation of the rule of reason is one that nature will not forgive.

In this view every act of every man is a moral act, to be tested by moral, and not by economic, criteria. Immoral means of acquiring goods are excluded. The enjoyment of the goods acquired is limited. The exclusion and the limitation are imposed by the nature of man and the nature of organized society. Personal and political rationalization subordinates economic rationalization by relating the material well-being of the individual first to the material well-being of his neighbor, and second to the highest good of the individual and of the whole society. The principle of the good of the person and the good of society is substituted for the principle of the largest returns at the lowest costs. Faith in asceticism and sacrifice is substituted for

46

asceticism :

faith in technology. An order based on charity is substituted for an order based on avarice.

The moral, intellectual, and spiritual reformation for which the world waits depends, then, upon true and deeply held convictions about the nature of man, the ends of life, the purposes of the state, and the order of goods. One cannot take part in this revolution if one believes that men are no different from the brutes, that morals are another name for the mores, that freedom is doing what you please, that everything is a matter of opinion, and that the test of truth is immediate practical success. Precisely these notions lie at the bottom of the materialism that afflicts us; precisely these notions are used in the attempt to justify man's inhumanity to man. The revolution to which we are called must end in the destruction of these notions and their power over individual and political action.

Those who are called most clearly to this revolution are the people of this country, who may yet have time. We must, by reconstructing our own lives, begin the reconstruction of economic, social, and political life. This means that we must reconstruct education, directing it to virtue and intelligence. It means that we must look upon economic activity, not as the end of life, but as a means of sustaining life, a life directed to virtue and intelligence. It means, too, that economic activity must be ordered to the common good, the good of the political society, the

47

aim of which is virtue and intelligence. It means, in short, the personal, rather than the economic, rationalization of life.

Every day that passes shows us what materialism has done and is doing to American education. The question most often put to me is: "What is wrong with our educational system?" The answer to this question is "Nothing." The educational system is operated by a million loyal and self-sacrificing individuals who have put on the greatest demonstration of mass education the world has ever seen. I can think of no criticism of them. On the contrary, they deserve the gratitude and support of the people.

The answer to the question asked me may, however, be given in somewhat more general terms. There is never anything wrong with the educational system of a country. What is wrong is the country. The educational system that any country has will be the system that country wants. It will be, in general, adapted to the needs and ideals of that country as they are interpreted at any given time. In the words of Professor Frank Knight, "Organized education, democratically controlled, is on its face, as regards fundamental ideals, an agency for promoting continuity, or even for accentuating accepted values, not a means by which 'society' can lift itself by its own bootstraps into a different spiritual world." Whatever is honored in a country will be cultivated there. A means of cultivating it is the educational system.

You may be sure, therefore, that the American educational system will be engaged in the cultivation of whatever is honored in the United States. Its weaknesses will be the weaknesses of American ideals. It may, of course, adopt methods of promoting those ideals that are not always adequate; but mistakes of this temporary kind will shortly be corrected. When experience shows that the people produced by the educational system do not honor what the country honors, ways will be discovered of manufacturing those who do.

If we look at the American democracy, we are struck by the fact that the infinite variety that was the chief characteristic of the democracies of Plato's day is missing from our own. De Tocqueville and Bryce devoted many pages to discussing the uniformity of American life. The democratic man is not as Plato saw him, filled with all desires and all interests. What he wants is financial success, and this produces the uniformity that has depressed foreign critics. We all know that in general the way to get ahead is to be safe and sound. Exhibitions of originality may make your superiors nervous. So De Tocqueville was finally forced to say: "I know of no country in which there is so little true independence of mind and freedom of discussion as in America." Such modifications as De Tocqueville would now have to make in this statement are the result of changes in other countries rather than our own.

I hope you will understand that, like all university presidents, I have a high opinion of money and am perfectly aware that without an adequate supply and distribution of it no civilization can exist. I am talking about that excessive, overwhelming, and primary urge for material goods that may be said to characterize our society. The discussion of social and political questions in this intellectual environment must revolve around the cost of doing anything about them. The cost of education is a valid objection to it if our people, including the educators, admit that financial success is the test of a good education. If any president of the United States were to regard the enrichment of the populace as his aim, he could not object to a discussion of his plans in terms of the outlay involved. The rich may legitimately complain at having their money taken away from them if the sole object of doing so is to make somebody else rich.

Since this is the setting in which American education operates, it is not enough, according to the prevailing theory, to develop the intelligence of the student so that he can cope with the problems of practical life. That kind of thing is too remote from the conditions of the economic struggle. What the pupil must have is some sort of strictly practical, technical training in the routines of a vocation that will enable him to fit into it with a minimum of discomfort to himself and his employer. The tendency is more and more to drive out of the course of study everything which is not immediately concerned with making a living.

Yet vocational education as we have understood it in this country is one of the methods of training where the means temporarily chosen by the educational system are not adequate to achieve the end in view. There is little evidence that vocational instruction of a strictly practical, technical, and routine kind is useful in enabling the graduate to fit into the vocation with any degree of success. As a matter of fact, instruction of this sort is likely to unfit him to meet the new and unforeseen problems raised by technology and social change. Rube Goldberg's cartoon of the boy who learned arithmetic for the wrong reason, namely, in order to add figures in a counting house, who found himself thrown out of work by the adding machine and who had no recourse except to slide down the banister rail toward an axe tied at the bottom, has a present or potential application to almost every gainful occupation. Think of the havoc that may yet be wrought among the stenographers of the nation, carefully trained in the public schools, if the dictaphone becomes the standard method of handling office correspondence. Think of the fate of California's beauticians if self-beautification for ladies becomes as simple a matter as it is for men. Or if this happy day shall not arrive, think what will happen in that great state when so many graduates of the University of California have been educated as beauticians that no one of them can make a living and there is nothing for them to do except to beautify one another gratis.

Of course young people must be trained in gainful occupations. The question is how. In industry 95 per cent of them are trained on the job. If this is regarded as too haphazard a procedure, an apprenticeship system can be instituted. Part-time arrangements, perhaps like those of the Engineering School at the University of Cincinnati, suggest a possible division of responsibility between education and industry. And when a student has actually entered a vocation something can be said for having him return to school for parts of the day or year to acquire further proficiency. This has been done in some states with local vocational agricultural schools. These devices, however, are quite different types of vocational education from those which assume that, beginning with infants, the school should attempt to give vocational instruction on a full-time basis under its own roof.

Vocational education has received new emphasis in the past ten years because of the changed situation the schools have confronted. Formerly, when a pupil failed, industry absorbed him. If he has failed lately, we have had to keep him still because he couldn't get a job. We haven't known what to do with him. He couldn't handle the present course of study, and we could think of nothing else except imitations of vocational activity. But I suggest that the problem here is one of communication, not of content. The standard curriculum still rests on reading. It is probably fair to say that most of the pupils who have failed up to now were pupils who could not read. We have made great progress in developing new methods of teaching reading. Perhaps if the schools used the best methods now available they could communicate with those whom they have been unable to reach so far. Certainly they could materially reduce the number of the functionally illiterate. It is doubtful whether they should rush into a vocational curriculum as an alternative to one that requires reading. We should try to frame a course of study that is good for any pupil and then focus our attention on developing the methods of transmitting it to those we cannot teach today.

A second consequence of American ideals in American education is that we have a tendency to base the curriculum on "useful" information. Ideas, which are, of course, the instruments of knowledge, do not seem particularly productive at first glance. If you can teach a boy how to become a second-rate bookkeeper, you have done something that is gratifying to him and satisfactory to you. To discuss with him the nature of justice, or the theory of the state, or the problem of truth, or the existence of God does not seem to have a very direct bearing on his economic future. If you succeed in modifying your and his financial interests somewhat and say that you are going to fit him into the contemporary world, you and he are likely to feel that the best way to do this is to give him lots of obsolescent information about the contemporary world. This is known as adjusting the young to their environment.

But if the aim of education is the communication of useful information, we may as well abandon the enterprise at once; for we shall be forced to the conclusion that Hendrik van Loon announced not long ago. He said: "In the present state of the world the educators might as well admit that there is no stable or valid knowledge that can be communicated to the young generation." Mr. van Loon is right: if knowledge is information about the contemporary scene, we should withdraw from education: there is no stable or valid knowledge that can be communicated to the young generation.

Certainly we shall have to withdraw from some vast and important areas of education, for many of them have nothing to do with useful information or vocational training. Take the fine arts and literature, for example. Though they have nothing to do with vocational training or information, we must teach them, because we vaguely feel that they must ornament any reputable curriculum. But when we teach them we cannot discuss the true or false.

There can be no principles to which we can resort. Therefore there are two standard methods that we employ: history and the communication of ecstasy. The historical method happily frees us from any consideration of the works themselves. We understand a poem by learning about the social, political, economic, and domestic conditions under which it was written. It is one of the conventions of the time. And it is to be understood in terms of the poverty, of the conjugal infelicity, or the ductless glands of its author.

The communication of ecstasy is less laborious for the teacher than the historical method; but it is likely to be even more wearing to the pupil. Reduced to its lowest terms it may be described in the words of one of my professors at Yale who told us that the excellence of a work of art could be measured by the thrill it sent down your spine. This may be called the chiropractic approach to literature. Persons with spines of peculiar rigidity or toughness would be denied the privilege of artistic comprehension, and an X-ray examination of the vertebrae would be a prerequisite to employment as a literary critic. At its best the communication of ecstasy leads to a certain appreciation of a work of art which lasts as long as the communicator is present, but which neither he nor his pupils can explain. This has a tendency to promote the development of private cults about the arts and to give support to the notion that in this field, at least, everybody is entitled to his own opinion.

A further consequence of current ideals in American education is that intellectual development is sacrificed to that practice in vocational techniques and that acquisition of information to which I have referred. The intellectual tradition in which we live receives merely incidental attention. There is no particular reason for talking about intellectual development if what you are concerned with is financial success, for there is little evidence of any correlation between the two. I do not deny that the law schools have manufactured some very crafty fellows and that the engineering schools have graduated some smart mechanics. I do deny that either the public schools or the universities are devoting themselves to producing people who have had genuine intellectual discipline and who have acquired those intellectual habits which the ancients properly denominated virtues.

As Mr. Butler of Columbia has said, "The youth thus deprived of the privilege of real instruction and real discipline is sent into the world bereft of his great intellectual and moral inheritance. His own share of the world's intellectual and moral wealth has been withheld from him. It is no wonder that the best use he can so often find to make of his time is to try, by whatever means he can devise, to share the material wealth of some of his fellows."

The vocational-informational philosophy of education that is coming to prevail is always defended on the ground that it is scientific, experimental, and liberal. On the contrary, he who proposes that education be concerned first of all with ideas, with principles, with the abiding and the permanent, is the true scientist and the true liberal. He is the true scientist because he understands the permanent questions with which science is concerned. He is the true liberal because he understands not merely the conventions of human society, but also the nature and possibilities of mankind. At the moment, those who hold that obsolescent information is the only proper study would have the greatest difficulty in criticizing the situation that obtained before the war in Italy. The trains, we are told, ran on time. The beggars had disappeared. There was less crime than there is in the United States. Italy had gained power and prestige. But it is only when we understand the nature of man that we can understand the nature of the state. And when we understand these we understand that the Italian state is not a state at all. It is an organization of force. It rests on a misconception of the purpose of the state. It denies the proper end of the person. It distorts the relation that should obtain between the person and the state. Standards of criticism, either in art or in politics, cannot be derived from vocational-informational studies.

As a result of our interest in vocational training and current information, there is today nothing to be taught except things obviously not worth teaching. Therefore, the general conclusion of anti-intellectuals is that we must have great men and women do the teaching. Only they can make the insignificant significant. If the student learns no subject matter, his life will at least be illuminated by the radiance of these great personalities. Pay no attention to what you should teach. Get Solomon in all his glory to sit behind the desk and your pupils will get an education.

I think they would. The trouble is that there is only one Solomon, and he has been a long time dead. What chance have ordinary teachers like us to light up the dark recesses of the cosmetic industry or enliven the reports of the Census Bureau? We have here in truth the formula of educational futilitarianism.

If the question is, then, What is wrong with the educational system? the answer is still: Nothing. If the question is, What can be done about what is wrong with American society? the answer is very difficult. Education provides the great peaceful means of improving society; and yet, as we have seen, the character of education is determined by the character of society. Still we must not assume a

58

defeatist attitude. The alternative to a spiritual revolution is a political revolution. I rather prefer the former. The only way to secure a spiritual revolution is through education. We must therefore attempt the reconstruction of the educational system, even if the attempt seems unrealistic or almost silly.

We must first determine what ideals we wish to propose for our country. I would remind you that what is honored in a country will be cultivated there. I suggest that the ideal that we should propose for the United States is the common good as determined in the light of reason. If we set this ideal before us, what are the consequences to the educational system? It is clear that the cultivation of the intellect becomes the first duty of the system. And the question, then, is how can the system go about its task? The only way in which the ideal proposed could ever be accepted by our fellow citizens and by the educational system would be by the gradual infiltration of this notion throughout the country. This can be accomplished only by beginning. If one college and one university—and only one—are willing to take a position contrary to the prevailing American ideology and suffer the consequences, then conceivably, over a long period of time, the character of our civilization may change.

I am asking you to think, therefore, what one college and one university might do to establish for the country and the educational system the ideal of the common good as determined in the light of reason. I suggest again that the primary object of institutions with this aim will be the cultivation of the intellectual virtues. I suggest that the cultivation of the intellectual virtues can be accomplished through the communication of our intellectual tradition and through training in the intellectual disciplines. This means understanding the great thinkers of the past and present, scientific, historical, and philosophical. It means a grasp of the disciplines of grammar, rhetoric, logic, and mathematics; reading, writing, and figuring. It does not, of course, mean the exclusion of contemporary materials. They should be brought in daily to illustrate, confirm, or deny the ideas held by the writers under discussion.

As Professor Whitehead has said, "Fundamental progress can be made only through the reinterpretation of basic ideas." This curriculum makes fundamental, rather than superficial, progress possible.

This program of general education is one to which all students, when they have learned to read, should be exposed. Those students who demonstrate in this period of general education that they have the intellectual qualifications for advanced work should be permitted to go on to the university, which I think of as beginning at about the present junior year. Those students who have not distinguished themselves or who do not wish to go on should be encouraged to betake themselves to practical life. This is the actual situation in every country of the world but this. In England, for example, not more than 40 per cent of the graduates of the great public schools like Eton, Harrow, and Rugby proceed to the university. The reason is that what establishes a boy's social position in England is attendance at a public school, which he leaves, ordinarily, at about the end of our sophomore year. Graduation from a university adds nothing to his acceptability. It is the old school tie that counts. In this country the moral equivalent of the old school tie is the bachelor's degree. I am in favor of awarding that degree as it is awarded in France and in French Canada, at the end of the period of general education, that is, at about the end of the sophomore year. I should hope that those students who have hitherto gone to college merely to confirm or acquire a social position could be induced to withdraw on receiving the document they came for. What has been done in this direction at the University of Chicago I shall set forth in the next chapter.

In a university we should have students interested in study and prepared for it. If the ideal of the country and of the educational system is the common good as determined in the light of reason, vocational instruction will disappear from the university. Courses designed solely to transmit information about current affairs will disappear as well. Such research as merely counting telephone poles will also vanish. Professors whose only interest is in dealing with immediate practical questions will vanish too. These excisions will leave us with a group of professors studying fundamental intellectual problems with students equipped to face them.

These intellectual problems fall roughly into three fields: those underlying problems that we call philosophical, including those called metaphysical and theological; those problems called scientific, including those raised by medicine and engineering; and those we find in the social sciences, including those presented by law and public administration.

The consideration of principles in these fields in a university might make these principles explicit. It might make the professors and students conscious of them. It might make them aware that these principles are ordering and clarifying. It would make them see that these principles, like all knowledge, are derived from experience. In the words of a mediaeval saint who was as sensible as he was saintly, "The human intellect is measured by things, so that a human concept is not true by reason of itself, but by reason of its being consonant with things, since *an opinion is true or false according as it answers to the reality.*" These principles, then, are refinements of common sense. They are methods of understanding and interpreting the symbols through which we know the environment. They are the basic ideas by the reinterpretation of which Mr. Whitehead believes fundamental progress may be made.

The graduates of a university so organized and so conducted should after three years of study have some rational conception of the common good and of the methods of achieving it. They might have learned how to use their heads. They might understand how to use them on the problems of the contemporary world. They might have established moral as well as intellectual standards. Their moral standards might endure because they would be based on reason and not on authority and precept alone. They would be aware of the intellectual tradition they had inherited. They should be consciously equipped with the intellectual instruments which we now unconsciously employ. They might be ready to take their place in a community devoted to the achievement of the common good through reason.

But we know that the United States is not a country devoted to the achievement of the common good through reason. We know that we are a people devoted to the acquisition of material goods by any means not too outrageous. What will be the fate, then, of our graduates? They will be, in my opinion, as well equipped for financial success as our graduates are today. But they may not want it; and they should be quite unwilling to use some popular methods of attaining it. ✳

I am afraid, therefore, that I am proposing some notable sacrifices on the altar of reform. The first few generations of graduates of my educational system might suffer the same fate as the martyrs of the early church. They might be that phenomenon horrible to American eyes, financial failures. Yet it is possible that if the one college and the one university for which I hope could persevere, the blood of martyrs might prove to be the seed of an enlightened nation. Like the early church this ideal college and this ideal university might gain strength, power, and influence. They might slowly alter the aspirations of our people. They might become a light to this country, and through it to the world.

IV

HOW TO SAVE THE COLLEGES

THE University of Chicago has lately been condemned by almost all the academic potentates in sight. It has been condemned by the Southern Association of Colleges and Secondary Schools, by the Association of American Colleges, by the National Conference of Church Related Colleges, by the North Central Association of Colleges and Secondary Schools, and by the American Association of University Women. Although individual educators have many times criticized the University of Chicago in the last fifty years, although they have attacked it for sponsoring the junior college, for introducing the quarter system, for abolishing course credits and required attendance at classes, and for abandoning intercollegiate football, this is the first time that full-dress assemblages of principalities and powers have publicly, officially, and formally deplored the University's conduct. This marks an all-time high in education deploring. The University must have done something very bad indeed.

What the University has done is to announce that

it will make it possible for students to get a liberal education by the end of the sophomore year and that it will award at that point, in recognition of their efforts, the degree traditionally associated with liberal education, namely the Bachelor of Arts.

Why is this bad? Offhand, it would appear highly desirable. Nobody has ever complained that college students work too hard. On the contrary, it is supposed that football and fun have consumed a large proportion of their waking hours. It has even been suggested that the course of study places so slight a strain on the energies of students that they are compelled to fill up their time with diversions which, if not intellectual, have at least the merit of being strenuous. It is believed that anybody can get into, stay in, and eventually graduate from some kind of college if he has the money to pay his bills. It has often been asserted on very high authority that the American educational system prolongs adolescence far beyond the point at which young people in other countries are turned out of education to assume adult responsibilities. In other countries this age is eighteen or nineteen; here the first honorable stopping place is at twenty-two. Hence the postponement of entrance upon adult careers, of professional study, and of marriage. Fortunate indeed is the young physician who can marry before he is thirty. Apparently the time is available in the educational system to complete liberal education by the age of twenty; and, if it can be done, there seem to be great advantages in doing it. The war emphasizes these advantages. The conscription age is twenty. If the members of the American community are to get a liberal education, which is the education every free citizen of a free community ought to have, they must get it by the time they are twenty years old. Can the American educational system be so perfect—or so inflexible— that it cannot make the adjustment necessary to give it to them? President Gannon of Fordham concludes, and the impartial observer must agree with him, that if the conscription age is lowered to eighteen it will be possible to give a liberal education even by that age. As Father Gannon has said, the degree should be given at that age if the education is complete at that age. The degree should follow the education, not the education the degree.

The degree now has little significance in terms of education. It is the recognition accorded a person who has passed through an eight-year elementary school, a four-year high school, and a four-year college. These institutions are regarded as fixed and immutable, to be eternally crowned by the bachelor's degree. What goes on in them is not important. The degree does not stand for education; it stands for a certain number of years in educational institutions, and this is not the same thing. Though what is done in those years is widely different from what

67

was done fifty or even twenty-five years ago, though there are almost as many different college programs as there are colleges, the same degree awaits the student now that awaited his father and grandfather, and it awaits him whether he goes to Harvard or the El Paso School of Animal Husbandry.

The United States Office of Education reports 1,072 institutions offering the bachelor's degree in the United States. Of this number, 485 had fewer than 400 students and 218 fewer than 200 students. Of the 713 privately supported colleges and universities that reported the amount of their endowment, 382 had less than $500,000. Many small colleges are first-class. They are small because they want to be. Some colleges without endowment are excellent. But many little, impoverished institutions are on the verge of financial and intellectual bankruptcy. The smallest and weakest of them give the same degree as Harvard, Columbia, California, and Yale.

The most striking development in American education in the last half century is the way in which the high school has taken over the college curriculum. Much of the education for which the bachelor's degree used to stand has now gone down into the high school. The colleges have filled up their last two years with specialized or professional work; but they have clung to the degree and have given it for the study of law, business, divinity, or anything else in which the student happened to spend his last two collegiate years. And this is the degree which once represented a liberal education.

Before the war the degree had lost its educational meaning. But it still had some meaning. It meant four years in some kind of college after the traditional high school. Now this meaning is gone. The colleges and universities are agreed on one thing: they must "accelerate" to permit their students to get as much education as they can before they are called into the armed forces. By eliminating holidays and vacations and by condensing courses many of them will make it possible for students to graduate from college two and a half years after entrance. Many of them will admit boys and girls who have not completed the senior year in high school. Many of them will give substantial credit to men called into the army. "Acceleration" sweeps away the last remnant of meaning which the bachelor's degree possessed.

If, then, the bachelor's degree has no meaning, why is the action of the University of Chicago, which is an attempt to give it meaning, so bad? The answer is that the degree is the symbol of the status quo. It is the symbol of the eight-year elementary school, the four-year high school, and the four-year college. It is the only thing that holds this system together. If you take away the degree, this system must fall apart—or reorganize. The degree has operated like a protective tariff in favor of this system. If it can be awarded at the end of the sopho-more year, then those committed to this system must face the educational problems they have been able to dodge. They must figure out what they are doing at each level and why. They must change the habits of their lives. Such suggestions are discon-certing.

What the academic potentates want to do is to keep things as they are. Hence the popularity of "acceleration." This process enables the institution to be patriotic, to help the student complete his work before he joins the army, and to do this with-out changing any of its habits except the vacations. This change is relatively painless to the professors, for most of them will be paid extra for teaching in the vacations. The colleges hope that it will be made painless for them by Federal subsidies to help the students pay their fees and even, perhaps, to help pay the professors. They would be paid to do what they are eager beyond anything to do, to main-tain the status quo.

With the world in dissolution the status quo can-not be maintained. But even if it could be, we should not attempt it. We should welcome the opportunity which the war gives us to rectify the American edu-cational system. The resolutions of the various edu-cational associations to which I have referred point with pride to the fact that the American four-year college and two-year junior college are unique:

"they have no exact counterpart" anywhere else in the world. This is elevating a mistake into an ideal. One might as well say that because Prohibition had no exact counterpart anywhere else in the world it was a fine temperance measure for the United States; or that because the American doughnut, or sinker, is unknown in Europe it is the perfect diet for our fellow citizens. Since human nature is everywhere the same, and since education has been going on from the time human beings first appeared on this planet, the uniqueness of an educational system is not a reason for pride but for concern. When we find, for example, that we complete education for citizenship from two to four years later than any other nation, we are justified in supposing that historical accidents, rather than superior sagacity, are responsible for the peculiarities of our educational system.

And this is in fact the case. At the root of our troubles lies the eight-year elementary school. This was a plain, everyday mistake. Horace Mann, who laid down the pattern of American education, admired the eight-year *Volksschule* of Germany. This was a terminal school; those who entered it were not supposed to go beyond it. Mann introduced it into the United States, where everybody is supposed to go beyond it. It is one thing to organize a school which is to give the pupil all the education he is ever going to get, and another to organize one which is to be the basis of a long educational career. In Europe and Great Britain those who are going into secondary education at all do so at around the age of eleven or twelve as compared with fourteen in the United States. If we had listened to Thomas Jefferson instead of Horace Mann we might have avoided this waste of time. Jefferson proposed to send the American child into secondary education at ten.

Since the eight-year elementary school was a historical accident, and one not adapted to the purpose it was expected to serve, it soon began to break up. By 1910 the junior high school had in many places split the twelve years of elementary and secondary school into six years of elementary school, three years of junior high school, and three years of senior high school. In these communities the young American entered upon secondary education at the age of twelve. But the four-year college remained untouched until the junior college movement, which started fifty years ago, began to take hold. It took hold fast. It accommodated freshmen and sophomores. It often conducted its work at public expense and in local high-school buildings, so that students were spared the cost of living away from home. There are now more than 600 junior colleges in the United States.

Many colleges and universities found it desirable to reorganize on the lines suggested by the junior

From
1943

72

college. They began to make a break between the
sophomore and junior years and one which they
often recognized by calling their freshman and
sophomore work a junior college or lower division
and their junior and senior work a senior college
or upper division. As early as 1909 the North Central Association of Secondary Schools and Colleges,
in attempting to say what a college was, began its
definition as follows: "The Standard American
College is a college with a four years' curriculum
with a tendency to differentiate its parts in such
a way that the first two years are a continuation
of, and supplement to, the work of secondary instruction as given in the high school, while the last
two years are shaped more and more distinctly
in the direction of special, professional, or university instruction." This is a frank statement that
the traditional four-year collegiate program had
broken down. It had no object of its own. It was
to supplement the high school at one end and the
professional school at the other.

But the four-year collegiate structure remained,
though the apartments in the building were vacant
or filled with tenants of a startlingly new variety.
What held it together was the B.A. degree. The
B.A. did more than preserve an archaic and dis-
integrating collegiate organization; it prevented
the development of an intelligent university organization. A university is an institution devoted to

advanced study, professional education, and research. It presupposes a liberal education and the
capacity to do independent intellectual work. A law
school, for example, should not be compelled to
teach its students to read and write or to train them
in good habits of study. Nor is there any evidence
that students who enter law school at age twenty-
two after graduation from college do any better
than those who enter at age twenty after two years
in college. In fact, most universities permit students
to devote all of their last college year to legal study,
and the University of Chicago Law School has for
a long time admitted men at the beginning of the
junior year in college.

University work, as distinguished from collegiate
work, can be begun at the beginning of the junior
year. If it can be, it should be. But in such a scheme
the B.A. degree loses meaning because it is awarded
for a mixture of liberal education and professional
study, or even for professional study alone. Since
the B.A. has lost all meaning anyway, this is not
a particularly serious matter. The plight of the
Master of Arts degree is a serious matter. This
degree is ordinarily awarded one year after the
B.A. and has come to mean little but the passage
of that one year. Students seek it because it is a
kind of union card needed in many states to get
a high-school teaching job. But it could stand for
something. If the B.A. were out of the way, con-

ferred at the end of liberal education, that is, at the end of the sophomore year, a three-year program to the M.A. could be developed which would give a real university education to those who were interested in and qualified for it. As the academic potentates never tire of saying, the bachelor's degree is universally recognized and time-honored. It is not universally recognized as meaning the same thing everywhere. It is not time honored in the sense that it is honored at one time for the same reasons as at another. But in this country it is recognized and honored as something everybody should have if he can scrape up the money to get it. This is just the trouble with it. Since it is conferred at the wrong point for the wrong reasons, it induces students to remain in college till the wrong point for the wrong reasons. Many students who should leave education at the end of the sophomore year stay on till the end of the senior year so that they can get the one recognizable and honorable reward that college offers.

Their presence gives the colleges the reputation of kindergartens and country clubs. It interferes with the education of those who are trying to get an education. It confuses the aims and functions of the higher learning. And the country is deprived of the useful work these young people might be doing instead of wasting their time in "college life." The national passion for the bachelor's degree

75

has been deplored for many years. The late Professor Barrett Wendell of Harvard saw no way to remedy the sad consequences of this passion except to confer the degree on every American citizen at birth. This proposal would be better than leaving it where it is. But a measure so extreme as Mr. Wendell's does not yet appear to be necessary. The degree can be given meaning and utility by making it stand for what it used to stand for, namely a liberal education, and by making it possible to complete such an education by the end of the sophomore year.

As many students are induced to stay in college who should not be there, so many students who are compelled to drop out of college are deprived of any recognizable and honorable reward for their educational efforts. Not many families can afford to keep their children out of active life until the age of twenty-two. President Rainey of the University of Texas has lately reported that 65 per cent of the entering freshmen at his institution do not continue beyond the end of the sophomore year. What is the educational situation of such young people in the traditional college or university? The curriculum which they have followed was not designed for them but for their more fortunate brothers and sisters who can stay four years. They have little which they can think of as an intelligible education. They have received no degree, or none

76

that is "universally recognized and time-honored." A plan of liberal education to be completed by the end of the sophomore year and the award of the bachelor's degree in recognition of it would give substance and significance to the college careers of these students.

With a six-year elementary school, a three- or four-year high school, and a three- or four-year college, we could bring the young American to the close of his formal liberal education and the B.A. degree by the age of eighteen or twenty. Such an organization the University of Chicago now has. The University operates a six-year elementary school, a four-year high school, and a four-year college. For the completion of the work of this four-year college the bachelor's degree will be conferred. For the time being, at least, students who have graduated from traditional high schools will be admitted to this college in the middle, that is, at the beginning of the conventional freshman year. They will be able to gain a mastery of the elements of a liberal education by the end of the sophomore year.

The potentates condemn this arrangement by calling it a two-year degree. But the question is not how long the student stays in college, but what he does there. The University of Chicago should be asked, not how many years its students take to the bachelor's degree, but what is the content of

ee represents. Not a
:ducational association
ication Chicago gives
'hey have not even in-

1ot a two-year degree,
are two-year degrees.
leges and universities
ing of the junior year
ing to the bachelor's
:nt of the students re-
o in any year have at-
istitutions. They have
:alaureate program in
new plan is a four-year
ith the junior year in
:d students from other
any time. To such stu-
:rtake to give the edu-
to have by the end of
:.

never found a layman
ntates say it is bad be-
1intaining institutions,
its. The layman, when
ly to think first of the
e potentates condemn
:y know that it is bad
o them to rebuild the

educational system in the interest of the students and the country.

The cry is that Chicago is ruining the colleges. On the contrary, Chicago is the hope of the colleges. The Chicago Plan shows how to meet the problems raised by the war and its aftermaths and how to do it, not by wild, makeshift dodges like "acceleration," but by a sound, long-term program which makes sense in war or peace.

The war will compel the reconstruction of American education. The war will compel us to justify every minute and every dollar that goes into education. It will squeeze the waste, water, and frivolity out of our educational system. It will force us to frame a plan of liberal education for every citizen and force us to make it available in such a way and at such a time that the citizen may complete it before he joins the army. It will mean that we must offer our people a scheme of education which commands our intellectual allegiance and which is entitled to theirs. As its contribution to the formulation of such a scheme the University of Chicago has developed its new program to the bachelor's degree.

V

EDUCATION AT WAR

IF you are going to war, you must know what you are willing to fight for. If you are going to defend territory, you must know what territory you are going to defend. If you are going to defend principles, you must know what your principles are and why you hold them. We may be fainthearted, even in defense of our native land, if we believe that the enemy is just as right as we are or that we are just as wrong as he.

We do not seem to get very far by talking about democracy. We know that Germany is not one. She says so. We know that Russia is not one, though Stalin says she is one. We are not sure about some elements in the government of England and France. We are not altogether sure about this country. The reason is, of course, that we do not know what a democracy is or grasp the fundamental notions on which it rests. We set out in the last war to make the world safe for democracy. We had, I think, no very definite idea of what we meant. We seemed then to favor a parliamentary system. No matter what the system concealed, if the system was there, it was democracy, and we were for it. Though Hitler is infinitely worse than the Kaiser, though the danger to the kind of government we think we believe in is infinitely greater than in 1917, we have less real, defensible conviction about democracy now than we had then. Too many so-called democracies have perished under the onslaught of an invader whose technical and organizing ability commands the admiration of a people brought up to admire technical and organizing skill. With our vague feeling that democracy is just a way of life, a way of living pleasantly in comparative peace with the world and one another, we may soon begin to wonder whether it can stand the strain of modern times, which, as our prophets never tire of telling us, are much more complicated than any other times whatever.

Is democracy a good form of government? Is the United States a democracy? If we are to prepare to defend democracy we must be able to answer these questions. I repeat that our ability to answer them is much more important than the quantity or quality of aeroplanes, bombs, tanks, flame-throwers, and miscellaneous munitions that we can hurl at the enemy. You may take it from Hitler himself. Rauschning reports him as saying: "Mental confusion, contradiction of feeling, indecisiveness, panic: these are our weapons." In view of the huge resources of this country, all that we have to fear is that the moral and intellectual stamina of the defenders will not be equal to the attack that has been made upon it.

Now democracy is not merely a good form of government; it is the best. Though the democratic ideal has long been cherished in this country, it has never been attained. Nevertheless, it can be attained if we have the intelligence to understand it and the will to achieve it. We must achieve it if we would defend democracy. J. Middleton Murry, an Englishman, said of England a year ago, "This country, as it is, is incapable of winning a Christian victory, because it simply is not Christian." Without passing on the specific application of this general principle, we can at least agree that the principle is sound and that no country can win a democratic victory unless it is democratic.

The reasons why democracy is the best form of government are absurdly simple. It is the only form of government that can combine three characteristics: law, equality, and justice. A totalitarian state has none of these, and hence, if it is a state at all, it is the worst of all possible states.

Men have reason, but they do not always use it. They are swayed by emotions and desires that must be held in check. Law is an expression of their collective rationality, by which they hope to educate and control themselves. Law is law only if it is an ordinance of reason directed to the good of the community. It is not law if it is an expression of

or collective reactivity —

82

passion or designed for the benefit of pressure groups. We have a government of men and not of laws when the cause of legislative enactments is anything but reason and its object anything but the common good.

The equality of all men in the political organization results inexorably from the eminent dignity of every individual. Every man is an end; no man is a means. No man can be deprived of his participation in the political society. He cannot be exploited or slaughtered to serve the ends of others. We have no compunctions about refusing animals the ballot. We have few about exploiting or slaughtering them in our own interest. But the human animal is bound to recognize the human quality of every other human animal. Since human beings, to achieve their fullest humanity, require political organization and participation therein, other human beings cannot deny them those political rights which human nature inevitably carries with it.

These same considerations help us to understand that the state is not an end in itself, as the Nazis think, or a mere referee, as the Liberty Leaguers used to say. Political organization is a means to the good of the community. And the common good itself is a means to the happiness and well-being of the citizens. The common good is peace, order, and justice, justice in all political, social, and economic relations. Justice is the good of the community. But what is the community? It is certainly something more than an aggregation of people living in the same area. A community implies that people are working together, and people cannot work together unless they have common principles and purposes. If half a crew of men are tearing down a house as the other half are building it, we do not say they are working together. If half a group of people are engaged in robbing, cheating, oppressing, and killing the other half, we should not say the group is a community. Common principles and purposes create a community; justice, by which we mean a fair allocation of functions, rewards, and punishments, in terms of the rights of man and the principles and purposes of the community, holds it together.

*The state, then, is not merely conventional, representing a compromise of warring interests who have finally decided that mutual sacrifices by subordination to a central authority are preferable to mutual extermination.*The state is necessary to achieve justice in the community. And a just society is necessary to achieve the terrestrial ends of human life.

We see, then, that we are back where we started. We began with the importance of principles in defense. We must now add that without principles and common principles clearly understood and deeply felt there can be no political community at all. There can be only a conglomeration of individuals wres-

tling with one another in the same geographical
region.

Let us inquire into what is needed if we are to
understand clearly and feel deeply the principles
on which democracy rests. What is the basis of these
principles of law, equality, and justice? In the first
place, in order to believe in these principles at all
we must believe that there is such a thing as truth
and that in these matters we can discover it. We are
generally ready to concede that there is truth, at
least of a provisional variety, in the natural sciences.
But there can be no experimental verification of the
proposition that law, equality, and justice are the
essentials of a good state. If there is nothing true
unless experiment makes it so, then what I have been
saying is not true, for I have not relied on any experimental evidence. But principles which are not
true are certainly not worth fighting for. We must
then agree that truth worth fighting for can be found
outside the laboratory.

Now truth is of two kinds, theoretical and practical. Theoretical truth tells us what is the case:
practical truth tells us what should be done. The
test of theoretical truth is conformity to reality. A
statement about the nature of man, for example,
is true if it describes man as he actually is. The test
of practical truth is the goodness of the end in view.
The first principle in the practical order is that men
should do good and avoid evil. The statement, for

down their lives in a
s just. The statement
gain power or wealth
lse.

ocracy, then, we must
ice between truth and
and wrong, and that
e objective standards
xperimentally verified.
s, rationalizations, or
believe that man can
right by the exercise
do so even as to those
e of the case, science

order to believe these
man has reason, that
alone, and that all his
n terms of his visceral
heritage. As Gilbert
man activities are the
at finding that by the
not marry his grand-
eve in democracy we
We must see that the
of men are the powers
t their end on earth is
ese powers. This in-
again, that there is a

difference between good and bad and that man is a rational animal. There is no use talking about moral powers if there is no such thing as morals, and none in talking about intellectual powers if men do not possess them.

Our great preoccupation today is freedom. When we talk about freedom we usually mean freedom from something. Freedom of the press is freedom from censorship. Academic freedom is freedom from presidents, trustees, and the public. Freedom of thought is freedom from thinking. Freedom of worship is freedom from religion. So too civil liberty, the disappearance of which throughout the world we watch with anxious eyes, is generally regarded as freedom from the state. This notion goes back to Rousseau. He located the natural man in a world of anarchy. The natural man had no political organization, and Rousseau strongly hinted that this was the most delightful aspect of his condition. The political state was a compromise, no less unfortunate because it was necessary. This view has been popular ever since. It is reflected every day in the attitude of those who look upon the activities of government as an evil. Though they admit that society must suffer certain necessary evils, they naturally have no wish to multiply them. Hence the attraction and power of the slogan: that government is best which governs least.

This notion of government and its role is based

on a myth, on a misconception of the nature of man and the nature of the state. It is not surprising that a doctrine absurdly grounded and workable only in countries of vast and untapped resources should contain in itself the seeds of an opposing doctrine, the doctrine that the state is all, that men are nothing but members of it, and that they achieve their ultimate fulfillment, not through freedom from the state, but through complete surrender to it. This is fascism. It ascribes to the political organization qualities that can belong only to God. It denies the eminent dignity of the person. It deprives man of the characteristic that raises him above the beasts, his reason. It sacrifices all that is specifically human, that is, moral, intellectual, spiritual development, and glorifies a specifically subhuman attribute, namely force.

These are the consequences of thinking of freedom as freedom from something. Freedom is not an end in itself. We do not want to be free merely to be free. We want to be free for the sake of being or doing something that we cannot be, or do unless we are free. We want to be free to obtain the things we want.

Now the things we want are good things. First, we want our private and individual good, our economic well-being. We want food, clothing, and shelter, and a chance for our children. Second, we want the common good: peace, order, and justice.

88

But most of all we want a third order of good, our personal or human good. We want, that is, to achieve the limit of our moral, intellectual, and spiritual powers. This personal, human good is the highest of all the goods we seek. As the private good, which is our individual economic interest, is subordinate to the common good, which is the interest of the community, so the common good is subordinate to our personal and human good and must be ordered to it. Any state in which the common good is sacrificed to private interests, or in which the moral, intellectual, and spiritual good of the citizens is sacrificed to the political organization is not a state. It is a fraud subsisting by force.

We in universities are concerned with free minds. How can we get them? We must remember that it is not freedom from something that we are seeking. We want minds that are free because they understand the order of goods and can achieve them in their order. The proper task of education is the production of such minds. But we can now see that we are not likely to produce them by following the recommendations of the more extreme of those called progressives in education. Freedom from discipline, freedom to do nothing more than pursue the interests that the accident of birth or station has supplied may result in locking up the growing mind in its own whims and difficulties.

The identification of freedom with lack of disroot of flower

act his attention

r adds, varying

all this type of

nselves as afloat

nart or compass

nuld not look to

gh the mazes of

ds by adopting

iplined progres-

ter luck by con-

ce of regarding

t events in the

pupils that we

tween 1942 and

n for the long

tes of 1941.

an achieve free

on making our

We want free

in their order.

ate economic in-

n and try to en-

When we say we want free minds we mean that we want minds able to operate well. The glory and the weakness of the human mind is that it is not determinate to certain things. It may range at will over the good and the bad. To be free to operate well, therefore, the mind requires habits that fix it on the good. So St. Augustine remarked that virtue, or good habits, is the right use of our freedom. What is needed for free minds is discipline, discipline which forms the habits which enable the mind to operate well. Nothing better can be said on this subject than the concise statement of John Dewey. "The discipline," he said, "that is identical with trained power is also identical with *freedom.*" The free mind is first of all the disciplined mind. The first step in education is to give the mind good habits.

The next step in the education of free minds is the understanding of what is good. The mind cannot be free if it is a slave to what is bad. It is free if it is enslaved to what is good. To determine the good and the order of goods is the prime object of all moral and political education. We cannot hope that one who has never confronted these issues can be either a good citizen or a good man. Yet today it is perfectly possible to attain to the highest reaches of the university without ever facing these questions. An educational system which does not make these questions the center of its attention is not an educational system at all. It is a large-scale housing venture. It may be effective in keeping young people out of worse places until they can go to work. It cannot contribute to the growth of free minds. It cannot help the rising generation solve the great problem of our time.

The great problem of our time is moral, intellectual, and spiritual. With a superfluity of goods we are sinking into poverty. With a multitude of gadgets we are no happier than we were before. With a declining death rate we have yet to discover what to do with our lives. With a hatred of war we are now deeply engaged in the greatest war in history. With a love of liberty we see much of the world in chains.

How can these things be? They can be because we have directed our lives and our education to means instead of ends. We have been concerned with the transitory and superficial instead of the enduring and basic problems of life and of society.

Since the freedom of autonomy is the end of human life, everything else in life should be a means to it and should be subordinate to it as means must be to ends. This is true of material goods, which are means, and a very necessary one, but not an end. It is true of the state, which is an indispensable means, but not an end. It is true of all human activities and all human desires: they are all ordered to,

92

and must be judged by, the end of moral and intellectual development.

The political organization must be tested by its conformity to these ideals. Its basis is moral. Its end is the good for man. Only democracy has this basis. Only democracy has this end. If we do not believe in this basis or this end, we do not believe in democracy. These are the principles which we must defend if we are to defend democracy.

Are we prepared to defend these principles? Of course not. For forty years and more our intellectual leaders have been telling us they are not true. In the whole realm of social thought there is nothing but opinion. Since there is nothing but opinion, everybody is entitled to his own opinion. There is no difference between good and bad; there is only the difference between expediency and inexpediency. We cannot even talk about good and bad states or good and bad men. There are no morals; there are only the folkways. Man is no different from the other animals; human societies are no different from animal societies. The aim of animals and animal societies, if there is an aim, is subsistence. The aim of human beings and human societies, if there is one, is material comfort. Freedom is simply doing what you please. The only common principle that we are urged to have is that there are no principles at all.

All this results in a colossal confusion of means

and ends. Wealth and power become the ends of life. Men become merely means. Justice is the interest of the stronger. This, of course, splits the community in two. How can there be a community between exploited and exploiters, between those who work and do not own and those who own and do not work, between those who are weak and those who are strong? Moral and intellectual and artistic and spiritual development are not with us the aim of life; they receive the fag ends of our attention and our superfluous funds. We seldom attempt to justify education by its contribution to moral, intellectual, artistic, and spiritual growth.

If everything is a matter of opinion, and if everybody is entitled to his own opinion, force becomes the only way of settling differences of opinion. And of course if success is the test of rightness, right is on the side of the heavier battalions. In law school I learned that law was not concerned with reason or justice. Law was what the courts would do. Law, says Hitler, is what I do. There is little to choose between the doctrine I learned in an American law school and that which Hitler proclaims.

Precisely here lies our unpreparedness. Such principles as we have are not different enough from Hitler's to make us very rugged in defending ours in preference to his. Moreover, we are not united and clear about such principles as we have. We are losing our moral principles. But the vestiges of them remain to bother us and to interfere with a thoroughgoing commitment to amoral principles. Hence we are like confused, divided, ineffective Hitlers. In a contest between Hitler and people who are wondering why they shouldn't be Hitlers the finished product is bound to win.

To say we are democrats is not enough. To say we are humanitarians will not do, for the basis of any real humanitarianism is a belief in the dignity of man and the moral and spiritual values that follow from it. Democracy as a fighting faith can be only as strong as the convictions which support it. If these are gone, democracy becomes simply one of many ways of organizing society, and must be tested by its efficiency. To date, democracy looks less efficient than dictatorship. Why should we fight for it? We must have a better answer than that it is a form of government we are used to or one that we irrationally enjoy.

Democracy is the best form of government. We can realize it in this country if we will grasp the principles on which it rests and recognize that unless we are devoted to them with our whole hearts democracy cannot prevail at home or abroad. In the great struggle that lies ahead, truth, justice, and freedom will conquer only if we know what they are and pay them the homage they deserve. This is the kind of preparedness most worth having, a kind without which all other preparation is worthless. This kind of preparedness has escaped us so far. It is our duty to our country to do our part to recapture and revitalize those principles which alone make life worth living or death on the field of battle worth facing.

The part of the universities in this effort is not, at first glance, entirely clear. Today, when my university has just celebrated its fiftieth anniversary, we must ask ourselves whether it is not already an anachronism. It rests on faith and hope, and presupposes a certain degree of economic stability. When faith is shaken and hope is dimmed and economic life disordered, the university may seem like an ornament of an age that is gone. It may arouse a certain nostalgic admiration, like a ruined abbey. It is beautiful. It is charming. It once had a place in society. But what is its function now?

How trivial now seem all the reasons for going to college, and hence for the existence of colleges, on which my generation was brought up: making friends, having a good time, getting plenty of fresh air and exercise, and advancing in the social or financial scale. I can even remember hearing from the president of a great university about the beneficent influence of collegiate Gothic on the aesthetic sensibilities of the young. These slogans may have sufficed in the carefree twenties. They will not do today.

The change in more fundamental matters is just as striking. The time of the founders of the University of Chicago was one of conscious or unconscious agreement upon the ultimate foundations of society and the ultimate purposes of the individual. Though men differed sharply, they differed not so much about their destination as about the methods of arriving at it. They would have been shocked to hear from any responsible person that morality was a matter of opinion, the state an end in itself, or God the product of wishful thinking. They did not need the warning of Socrates that the unexamined life was no life for man, because the examination had been conducted long before, and its results were imbedded in the tradition which guided the daily actions of men. The American university did not need to reformulate the ideals which should animate mankind, and still less to suggest that ideals were important. All that was needed, men thought, was more knowledge to enable them to reach the goals which they more or less clearly had before them. The university would supply the means to improve a civilization the main lines of which were laid down and the aims of which were taken for granted by those who enjoyed its blessings.

In those areas in which the last half century has brought no change in the fixity and clarity of beliefs the American university has surpassed the highest hopes of its founders. People still want material goods; and through the natural sciences we can now produce a range and luxuriance of such goods that would embarrass a Roman emperor. People still want health; and through the American university we may sometime achieve a longevity comparable to that of the heroes who flourished before the Flood. <u>Wherever we know what we want, wherever we want it badly enough, the American university can help us get it.</u>

But we still vaguely feel that there are other goods beyond bodily and external goods; and we are no longer in conscious or unconscious agreement on the nature and existence of the other goods beyond. The last half century has substituted confusion and bewilderment for the simple faith in the light of which the universities carried on their work. The civilization which we thought so well established seems on the verge of dissolution. The religious belief which led so many denominations to found universities does not sustain their constituencies today. Instead of feeling that we were born with a common inheritance of ideas about the purpose of the state and the destiny of man, we listen to competing affirmations of contradictory positions on these issues without being able either to accept or deny them in a manner satisfactory to ourselves.

Since we are confused about ends, we do not know how to employ means. Though our means of improving the material conditions of existence exceed those of any previous generation, we could not use them, in the great depression, to protect our fellow citizens from starvation and despair. The means of improving the material conditions of existence are now diverted to the extermination of mankind on a greater scale than ever before.

Gibbon, in his celebrated chapter summarizing the reasons for the fall of the Western Empire, relieves the fears of Europe by saying that there will never be another barbarian conqueror. His reason is simple. War now requires the knowledge of a large number of arts and sciences. Hence to excel in war the barbarian must cease to be barbarous. Since man first discovered how to master the forces of nature all history has been tending toward this goal. Gibbon's final remark is, "We may therefore acquiesce in the pleasing conclusion that every age of the world has increased and still increases the real wealth, the happiness, the knowledge, and perhaps the virtue of the human race."

The conclusion is pleasing; the premise is false. Professor Nef's researches show that the rate of increase of real wealth is rapidly declining. Though knowledge has grown from more to more, happiness and virtue have not. And we see that a barbarian conqueror equipped with knowledge can be more barbarous, as well as more dangerous, than any of his unlettered predecessors.

The centrifugal forces released through the dissolution of ultimate beliefs have split the universities into a thousand fragments. When men begin to doubt whether there is such a thing as truth or whether it can ever be discovered, the search for truth must lose that precision which it had in the minds of those who founded the American universities. And if the traditional notion of freedom, when dragged up out of our subconscious, looks less impressive than we had always supposed it would, free inquiry ceases to be that infallible guide to terrestrial salvation which our academic ancestors thought it was. We must now confess that the beacons established to illuminate the pathway of our people give a light that is flickering and dim. The universities, instead of leading us through the chaos of the modern world, mirror its confusion.

If the members of universities are now to do for their own day what their academic ancestors did for theirs, they will have to continue what their ancestors did, and they will have to do something more. They will have to recapture, revitalize, and reformulate for our time the truths which gave purpose and significance to the work of their predecessors. We are in the midst of a great moral,

intellectual, and spiritual crisis. To pass it success-
fully or to rebuild the world after it is over we
shall have to get clear about those ends and ideals
which are the first principles of human life and of
organized society. Our people should be able to
look to the universities for the moral courage, the
intellectual clarity, and the spiritual elevation
needed to guide them and uphold them in this
critical hour. The universities must continue to
pioneer on the new frontiers of research. But today research is not enough either to hold the university together or to give direction to bewildered
humanity. We must now seek not knowledge alone,
but wisdom.

This is what the University Grants Committee
of England meant when it said, "Here arises the
responsibility of the universities. They are the in-
heritors of the Greek tradition of candid and
intrepid thinking about the fundamental issues involved in the life of the individual and of the
community, and of the Greek principle that the
unexamined life is no life for man."

Candid and intrepid thinking about fundamental
issues—in the crisis of our time this is the central
obligation of the universities. This is the standard
by which they must be judged. This is the aim
which will give unity, intelligibility, and meaning
to their work. This is the road to wisdom. Upon
that road the American university will regain its

own soul and bring hope and comfort to a distracted world.

In this view the university is a symbol. As such, its importance is greater than at any time in its history. The celebration of its ideals was never so necessary as now. The light it has shed since earliest antiquity is now extinguished in almost the whole of Europe. With the whole world in flames we must raise a standard to which all honest and right-thinking men can repair, to which embattled humanity can rally. It is the standard of freedom, truth, and reason. To the forces of brutality, chaos, and ignorance the university opposes the power of righteousness, order, and knowledge. Upon the triumph of that power the survival of Western Civilization depends.

An ancient sage remarked that the state came into being for the sake of life, for mutual assistance and protection. It made mere living possible. But, he went on, the state continued in existence for the sake of the good life, to develop and perfect through common effort the noblest abilities of all the citizens. We can see the analogy in education. Education must exist for the sake of mere life. Every citizen must be able to read, at least enough to see "Danger" on a sign or "Poison" on a bottle. Every citizen must be able to count, or his difficulties in paying his fare may impede the movements of others. Every citizen must discover somehow that some diseases are contagious and that intimacy with a sufferer from smallpox is unwise. Every citizen must learn, in the educational system or out of it, whatever he has to learn in order to earn a living, so that he will not starve to death from sheer incompetence. These things are necessary for mere life. Even the modern dictator must see to it that his subjects acquire this kind of education. But as all modern dictators have shown, they cannot tolerate a university devoted to candid and intrepid thinking. The reason is that such a university is the symbol of the good life. A good life is a life directed to knowing the truth and doing justice. It is impossible without freedom of action and freedom of thought. Freedom, truth, and justice would be fatal to the totalitarian state. They are the aspirations of democracy. The university can symbolize these aspirations in the United States.

Yet at the time when candid and intrepid thinking is more necessary than ever it is harder than ever to carry it on. The universities are now instrumentalities of total war. The obligation pressed most urgently upon them is that of conducting research on military secrets, of training men and women for war, and of housing and feeding members of the armed forces.

"Whither is fled the visionary gleam?
Where is it now, the glory and the dream?"

My answer is that the basic function of the universities is candid and intrepid thinking about fundamental issues. Other tasks have now been imposed upon them which will make it difficult, perhaps very difficult, perhaps impossible, to perform their basic function. The degree of difficulty will depend on the length and intensity of the war. But the effort to perform the basic function must be made.

Victory cannot save civilization. It can merely prevent its destruction by one spectacular method. Since civilization was well on its way to destruction before the war began, success in the war will not automatically preserve it. The domination of the world by England, the United States, and Russia is not identical with civilization. The victory of these powers gives mankind a better chance to be civilized than their defeat. Whether or not mankind will take that chance depends on the kind of intellectual, moral, and spiritual leadership it has.

Civilization is not a standard of living. It is not a way of life. Civilization is the deliberate pursuit of a common ideal. Education is the deliberate attempt to form human character in terms of an ideal. The chaos in education with which we are familiar is an infallible sign of the disintegration of civilization; for it shows that ideals are no longer commonly held, clearly understood, or deliberately pursued. To formulate, to clarify, to vitalize the ideals which should animate mankind—this is the incredibly heavy burden which rests, even in total war, upon the universities. If they cannot carry it, nobody else will; for nobody else can. If it cannot be carried, civilization cannot be saved. The task is stupendous. But we must remember the words of William the Silent: "It is not necessary to hope in order to undertake, or to succeed in order to persevere." With determination, energy, unselfishness, and humility the universities must struggle to meet the challenge of our time.

was upon the univer...
dollars was still th...
Harvard. A thousand...
superstitious. But to...
William the Schola...
tutor of undergrad...
system. When the la...
and probably the wo...
the challenge of our...

APPENDIX

The first lecture foundation in the Graduate School of Louisiana State University was established in 1933, and named "The Edward Douglass White Lectures on Citizenship" in honor of one of Louisiana's greatest sons who, as United States Senator from Louisiana and Chief Justice of the United States, brought distinction and honor both to public life and to the profession of law of which he was a member. Each year a distinguished scholar or statesman is invited to give lectures dealing with problems of citizenship to stimulate a broader interest in public affairs and to interpret ideals of democracy based upon principles of law and justice and peace.

The Edward Douglass White Lectures have been given by Howard W. Odum, Kenan Professor of Sociology and Director of the Institute for Research in Social Science at the University of North Carolina, on "New Frontiers of Citizenship" (1933); Manley O. Hudson, Bemis Professor of International Law at Harvard University, on "Three Pacts of Peace" (1935); William Y. Elliott, Chairman of the Department of Government at Harvard University, on "The Future of the Constitution" (1936); Thomas Reed Powell, Langdell Professor of Law at Harvard University and President of the American Political Science Association, on "Some Ways of a Written Constitution" (1937); Herman Finer, Head of the Department of Public Administration, and Chairman of the Board of Administration and Examiners for the University Diploma in Public Administration at the London School of Economics and Political Science, on "The State in the Twentieth Century" (1938); Robert Morrison MacIver, Lieber Professor of Political Philosophy and Sociology and Executive Officer of the Department of Social Science at Columbia University, on "The New Leviathan: the State in Crisis" (1939); Frank Porter Graham, President of the University of North Carolina, on "Some Problems of Freedom and Democracy in the Modern World" (1940); and Robert M. Hutchins, Chancellor of the University of Chicago, on "Citizenship and Education" (1941).

Professor MacIver's lectures were published by the Louisiana State University Press in 1939 under the title "Leviathan and the People."

Dr. Hutchins' lectures are presented in this volume, with two additional chapters, "The Autobiography of an Uneducated Man" and "How to Save the Colleges."